SCOTTISH PROVERBS

Nicola Wood

Chambers

© Nicola Wood, 1989

Published by W & R Chambers Ltd Edinburgh, 1989
Reprinted 1989

British Library Cataloguing in Publication Data
Wood, Nicola
    Scottish proverbs.—(Chambers mini guides)
    1. Proverbs in English. Scottish proverbs.
    Anthologies
    I. Title
    398'.9'21

    ISBN 0-550-20052-5

Cover design by John Marshall

Typeset by Bookworm Typesetting Ltd, Edinburgh
Printed in Singapore by
Singapore National Printers Ltd

Contents

Preface

It has been my intention, in compiling what is really quite a small collection of proverbs, to provide just a sample of this rich core of Scottish tradition. Andrew Henderson, in his *Scottish Proverbs*, quotes Lord Bacon as saying 'The genius, wit and spirit of a nation are discovered in their proverbs'. The Scots were long, and justly, famed for their pithy observation of life and their pawky humour, expressed in proverb form, and although the form itself is not now in such common use, the Scots have not lost their ability to look at life sideways and laugh at themselves.

The proverbs I have selected are, as far as possible, purely Scots, but many sayings are common to several languages and these are also well represented in this book.

I have greatly enjoyed the hours I have spent reading the many collections of proverbs gathered by scholars, who have often made it a lifetime's work, and I can only hope that you will enjoy the fruit of my labour as much.

There is not much to say about the use of this book, as the lay-out is very simple. The arrangement is alphabetical, for it is impossible to categorise proverbs satisfactorily and I am sure readers would have disagreed constantly with my interpretation, had I attempted this form. There is a glossary, which some may say is insultingly full for Scots readers. It is my cherished hope, however, that the readership of this compilation will not be purely Scots. In any event, some Scots are not as Scots as they might be, and they may also find the glossary helpful. Finally, I must express my thanks to Forbes MacGregor, the author of *Scottish Proverbs and Rhymes*, some of whose anecdotes I have included to illustrate proverbs.

Nicola Wood

Scottish Proverbs

A

A' ae oo.

Literally – all one wool.
It's all to the same end.

A' are gude lasses, but where do the ill wives come frae?

A' are no friends that speak us fair.

Don't trust somebody just because he compliments you.

A bad wound may heal, but a bad name will kill.

But – sticks and stones may break my bones but words will never hurt me.

A bairn maun creep afore it gangs.

Learn basic facts before you attempt anything ambitious.

A bauld fae is better than a cowardly friend.

A bawbee cat may look at a King.

A bird in the hand's worth twa
fleeing by.

A black shoe mak's a blythe
heart.

A shoe seen to be blackened by hard work
will ensure the supply of work goes on and
its wearer remains happy.

A blate cat makes a prood moose.

A blind man needs nae looking-
glass.

A blind man's wife needs nae
painting.

A bonny bride is sune buskit
And a short horse is sune wispit.

A pretty bride needs little decoration;
a small horse little grooming.

A bonny gryce may mak an ugly
soo.

Beauty fades with the passing of time.

About the moon there is a brugh: the weather will be cauld and rough.

The halo seen about the moon may well mean bad weather.

A broken kebbuck gangs sune dune.

A broken cheese is as good as eaten.

A careless watch invites the thief.

A' cats are grey i' the dark.

A cauld needs the cook as muckle as the doctor.

Feed a cold!

'A clean thing's kindly', quo' the wife when she turned her sark after a month's wear.

A relief for this wife's close friends, no doubt.

A close mouth catches nae flees.

Keep your mouth shut and you'll stay out of trouble.

A cock's aye crouse on his ain midden-head.

It's easy to be brave on your own territory.

A coward's fear makes a brave man braver.

A' cracks mauna be trewed.

Don't believe all you hear.

A' craiks a' bears.

Great complainers wish to make everyone believe they have a hard life.

A craw will no wash white.

Nor can the leopard change its spots.

A crook in the Forth is worth an earldom in the North.

An unkind jibe about the value of unproductive northern lands.

A croonin' coo, a crawlin' hen and a whistlin' maid are ne'er very chancy.

Young girls were told that whistling was neither attractive nor natural.

A dink maiden aft maks a dirty wife.

A 'dink' girl often forgets her 'dinkiness' after marriage.

A dish o' married love richt sune grows cauld.
And dozens doon to nane as folks grow auld.

A dog winna yowl if ye fell him wi' a bane.

Pelt a dog with bones and he won't complain.

A doucer man ne'er brak warld's bread.

An expression of unqualified respect.

A drap and a bite's but sma' requite.

Friends are always welcome at our table.

A drink is shorter than a tale.

An excuse for a drink while a story is being told.

A dumb man hauds a'.

Ae hauf o' the warld disna ken how the ither hauf lives.

Ae hour i' the morning is worth twa at night.

A greedy ee ne'er got a gude pennyworth.

A gude friend is worth mony relations.

A gude goose may hae an ill gaislin.

A horn spune hauds nae poison.

Humble people tend to be honest.

A hungry man's meat is lang o' makin' ready.

So it seems.

A' is no gowd that glisters, nor maidens that wear their hair.

All that glistens is not gold.
Time was, in Scotland, when virgins 'wore their hair' or wore no headdress. The speaker casts doubt on the honesty of some who went about bareheaded.

A kiss and a drink o' water mak a wersh breakfast.

A girl's charms were obviously not enough for this man.

A man's a man for a' that.

The refrain of Robert Burns' song.
All men are basically the same.

Ane may like the kirk well enough and no ride on the riggin' o't.

A poke at fanatical church-goers.

As daft as a yett on a windy day.

A toom pantry maks a thriftless gude-wife.

The housewife cannot practise the virtue of thrift unless she has food in her pantry to begin with.

Auld sparrows are ill to tame.

It's hard to teach an old dog new tricks.

Auld wives were aye guid maidens.

They always claim this.

B

Bad legs and ill wives should stay at hame.

They're both a nuisance when you want to enjoy yourself.

Bairns are certain care, but nae sure joy.

Bairns speak i' the field what they hear i' the ha'.

Don't tell confidences when children are about.

Bannocks are better than nae breid.

Something is better than nothing at all.

Beauty's muck when honour's tint.

Beauty is worthless when honour is lost.

Be aye the things ye would be ca'd.

Do as you would be done by.

'Because' is a woman's reason.

'I have no other but a woman's reason.
I think him so, because I think him so'.
Shakespeare.

Bees that hae honey in their mouths hae stings in their tails.

Watch out for smooth talkers.

Beg frae beggars and you'll ne'er be rich.

Begin with needles and preens, and end wi' horn'd nowte.

A small deceit may lead to a larger one.
Used as a caution against dishonesty.

Believe a' ye hear, an' ye may eat a' ye see.

Be ready wi' your bonnet, but slow wi' your purse.

The legendary Scotsman: lift your hat
politely, but you don't have to pay for
everything.

Best to be off wi' the auld love before ye be on wi' the new.

Very sound advice.

Be thou weel, or be thou wae,
Thou wilt not aye be sae.

Better bairns greet than bearded men.

This was used when punishment was handed out.

The story goes that John Knox made Mary, Queen of Scots cry in his attempts to convert her to Protestantism and used this saying, substituting 'women' for 'bairns'.

Better mak your feet your freends.

Run away.

Better wear shune than sheets.

It is better to be healthy and using up expensive shoe-leather than in bed.

Butter to butter's nae kitchen.

Used when women greeted each other with a kiss, implying it was rather a waste without a man on one side of it.

C

Ca' a cow to the ha' and she'll rin to the byre.

People are more comfortable in familiar surroundings.

Ca' again, ye're no a ghaist.

Come again, you're welcome.

Ca' canny, and ye'll break nae graith.

Go carefully and all will be well.

Ca' canny, lad, ye're but a new-come cooper.

Caff and draff is gude enough for aivers.

Ordinary food suits ordinary people.

Ca'ing names breaks nae banes.

Canna has nae craft.

A unwilling person will never learn.

Cast a cat ower the hoose and she'll fa' on her feet.

Some people are always lucky.

Cast not a cloot till May be oot.

Don't discard winter clothing until May-blossom is out.

Cats and carlins sit i' the sun, but fair maidens sit within.

Girls should be pale and interesting, not suntanned.

Chalk's no shears.

Proposing something is not actually doing it. Tailors mark cloth with chalk before they cut it.

Charity begins at home, but shouldna end there.

Choose your wife on Saturday, not Sunday.

A wife should be chosen on a working day, (for her usefulness in the home, not for her Sunday appearance, i.e. in fine dress and on her best behaviour.)

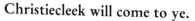

Christiecleek will come to ye.

Used by mothers to frighten their naughty children.

Christie was the leader of a cannibal gang, forced to this horror by the privations of the 14th century. He attacked his victims with a hook or 'cleek' and so earned his name. He was apparently never caught and eventually returned to a perfectly respectable life.

Come a' to Jock Fool's house and ye'll get bread and cheese.

Spoken sarcastically of those who will invite anybody to their house.

Creep before ye gang.

Curses mak the tod fat.

It's no use just complaining; do something about it.

D

Daffin' does naething.

Playing accomplishes nothing.

Daily wearin' needs yearly beiting.

Things in constant use need constant renewal.

Danger past, God forgotten.

Daughters and dead fish are kittle keepin' wares.

Daughters should be married and dead fish eaten, because they both spoil on the hands of their keepers.

Dawted daughters mak' daidlin wives.

Spoiled daughters make indifferent wives.

Daylight will peep through a sma' hole.

Where there's light, there's hope.

Death and drink-draining are near neighbours.

A reference to the partying that went on after a funeral – or an early demonstration of the dangers of drinking?

Death comes in and speirs nae questions.

Deil be in the house that ye're beguiled in.

A compliment, meaning that a person is so shrewd, only the devil could fool him.

Deil mend ye if your legs were broken.

Not a compliment. The speaker wishes nothing but evil on his listener.

Did ye ever fit counts wi' him?

Don't trust a friend until you've had money dealings with him.

Ding doon the nest and the rooks will flee awa.

Destroy a villain's hide-out and he'll run away.
This proverb was applied at the Reformation, when many abbeys and cathedrals were destroyed.

Dinna gut your fish till ye get them.

Don't count your chickens before they're hatched.

Dinna scaud your mouth wi' other folk's kail.

Don't gossip!

Dinna sigh for him, but send for him: if he's unhanged, he'll come.

Don't waste your time wishing for something, get it done.

Dinna tell your fae when your foot sleeps.

Dinna touch him on the sair heel.

Don't talk to him on a subject you know to be sensitive.

Dit your mouth wi' your meat.

A suggestion intended to put a stop to gossip.

Do a man a good turn, and he'll never forgie ye.

It's hard to owe someone a favour.

Do't by guess, as the blind man fell'd the dog.

Do well, an' doubt nae man; do ill, an' doubt a' men.

Honesty is the best policy.

Do your turn weel, and nane will speir what time ye took.

Work should be done well, rather than hastily.

Draff he soucht, but drink was his errand.

He asked for one thing, but really wanted another.

Dry bargains bode ill.

Time was when a bargain not sealed by a drink was considered unlucky.

E

Eagles catch nae flees.

Spoken of conceited people who ignore small details.

Early sow, early mow.

East or West, hame is best.

Easy learning the cat the road to the kil~

When y   natural bias is in a particular direction   's easy to follow your own inclinatic

Eat and well come, fast and twice as well come.

Eat-weel's Drink-weel's brither.

Good drinking goes with good eating.

Eild and poortith are a sair burden for ae back.

Eith keeping the castle that's no besieged.

Life is easy when all goes well.

Even a haggis will run downhill.
Spoken of a cowardly action.

Every craw thinks his ain bird whitest.

Every man bows to the bush he gets beild frae.
Every one pays homage to his protector.

Every man can guide the ill wife weel but him that has her.

Every man for himself, and God for us a'.

Every man for his ain hand, as Henry Wynd fought.
Two clans fought a battle with 30 men a side, about the year 1392. When one man went missing, his place was taken by a small bandy-legged man called Henry Wynd. He made a great contribution to the fighting, but didn't know which side he was on.

Every man has his ain bubbly-jock.

Everyone has his own problems.

A half-wit working for a farmer was asked if he was contented, by a visitor. He admitted he was well-fed and looked after, but was very upset because the turkey had an aversion to him and chased him every time he saw him.

Every man's man had a man, and gar'd the Threave fa'.

Threave Castle was very strong and belonged to the Black Douglases. The governor left a deputy, who, in turn, left a substitute in charge. This final substitute was incompetent and the castle was taken. The lesson is clear.

Every man to his taste, as the man said when he kiss'd his cow.

Everything has its time, and sae has a ripplin'-kame.

There is a proper time for everything.

Experience keeps a dear school, but fools will learn in nae ither.

F

Facts are chiels that winna ding.
Facts cannot be denied.

Faint heart ne'er wan fair lady.

Fair exchange is nae robbery.

Fair fa' gude drink, for it gars folk speak as they think.
Not always such a good thing!

Fair fa' you, and that's nae fleeching.

Fair maidens wear nae purses.
Girls were never allowed to pay in mixed company.

Fair words winna mak the pot boil.

Fann'd fires and forced love ne'er dae weel.

Far ahint maun follow the faster.

Far awa fowls hae fair feathers.

The further away and the more unattainable something is, the more attractive it becomes.

Far frae my heart's my husband's mother.

Have mothers-in-law ever been popular?

Far sought and dear bought is gude for ladies.

You will be looked on with favour if you go to a lot of trouble.

Feckless fools should keep canny tongues.

Silly or mischievous people should be careful what they say.

Fleas and girning wives are waukrife bedfellows.

Not a recommendation for marriage.

Fools look to tomorrow; wise men use tonight.

Better not to postpone what you can do now.

Fools mak feasts and wise men eat them.

An impertinent guest of the Duke of Lauderdale is supposed to have made this comment. The Duke then retorted 'Aye, and wise men mak proverbs and fools repeat them'.

Fools see ither folk's faults and forget their ain.

For a tint thing, carena.

For want o' a steek a shoe may be tint.

A stitch in time saves nine.
Look after your property and your business carefully.

Frae saving comes having.

Frae the teeth forward.

He speaks from the lips only, and is not sincere.

Friday flit, short time sit.

It was considered unlucky to move house on a Friday.

G

Gardener's law – Eat your fill, but pouch nane.

Gathering gear is weel liket wark.

Acquiring wealth is a pleasant pastime.

Gather haws before the snaws.

Gaunting bodes wanting ane o' things three, sleep, meat or gude companie.

Gaunting gaes frae man tae man.

Gaylie would be better.

Upon feeling ill, as 'pretty well' would be better.

Get what you can, and keep what you hae, that's the way to get rich.

Gie a bairn his will, and a whelp his fill,
and nane o' them will e'er do weel.

Don't spoil your children.

Gie a beggar a bed and he'll pay ye wi' a loose.
Don't do favours for good-for-nothings.

Gie him a hole, and he'll find a pin.
Give him a chance and he'll take it.

Gie him an inch, and he'll take an ell.

Gie is a gude fellow, but he soon wearies.
One tires of always giving.

Giff-gaff maks gude friends.
Give and take between people leads to friendship.

Glib i' the tongue is aye glaiket at the heart.
A smooth tongue is a sign of a deceitful heart.

Glum folk's no easily guided.
Sullen people are difficult to cope with.

God keep the cat out o' our gate, for the hens canna flee.

God's aye kind to fu' folk and bairns.

A comment on the miraculous way that drunkards avoid injury.

God sends meat and the deil sends cooks.

God send ye mair sense and me mair siller.

Great pains and little gains soon mak a man weary.

Greed is envy's auldest brither: scraggy wark they mak thegither.

Gude health is better than wealth.

Said with a touch of wistfulness?

H

Ha' binks are sliddry.

Literally – the benches in the manor-house are slippery.
The favours of your betters are uncertain.

Had you sic a shoe on ilka foot, you would shochel.

If you had my problems, you'd be miserable too.

Hae God, hae a'.

Hain'd gear helps weel.

Saved money is a help.

Half acres bear aye gude corn.

People who have little take good care of it.

'Hame's hamely', quo the deil when he found himself in the Court of Session.

Lawyers were never considered saintly.

Hang a thief when he's young and he'll no steal when he's auld.

Hap an' a ha'penny is warld's gear enough.

Happiness and moderate means in this world are enough.

Happy man be his dool.

A good wish – that happiness may be his greatest misfortune.

Happy's the maid that's married to a mitherless son.

More bad press for mothers-in-law.

Happy the man that belongs to nae party, but sits in his ain house, and looks at Benarty.

Sir Michael Malcolm of Loch Ore said this as an old man, on hearing talk of the French Revolution. It seems a very sensible attitude. Benarty is a hill.

Haste maks waste, and waste maks want, and want maks strife between the gudeman and the gudewife.

Hauf a tale is eneugh for a wise man.

He jumped at it, like a cock at a grosset.

He accepted it eagerly.

He needs a lang spune that sups kail wi' the deil or a Fifer.

Only the devil was as wily as a man from Fife.

He rides sicker that never fa's.

It's a perfect man who never makes mistakes, i.e. this is an impossibility.

He's as bold as a Lammermuir lion.

The Lammermuir Hills are not noted for their lions, but sheep are thus nicknamed locally.

He's either a' honey or a' dirt.

He is either very kind or very unkind.

He's horn deaf on that side o' his head.

He is wilfully deaf on that subject.

He stumbles at a strae and lowps ower a linn.

When it suits him, he finds problems.

He that blaws in the stoor fills his ain een.

If you make trouble, don't expect to escape it yourself.

He that eats but ae dish seldom needs the doctor.

In praise of moderation.

He that has a muckle neb thinks ilka ane speaks o't.

**He that looks wi' ae ee, and winks wi' anither,
I wouldna believe him, though he was my brither.**

Winking is not the habit of a trustworthy man.

He would skin a louse for the talla.

He is a miser.

He would tine his lugs if they werena tacked to him.

He is very forgetful.

High trees show mair leaves than fruit.

A jibe against tall people.

His head will never fill his faither's bonnet.

He will never be as clever as his father.

Hunger's good kitchen to a cauld potato, but a wet divot to the lowe o' love.

If you are hungry, you will eat anything, but you won't be in a mood for romance.

I

I ance gie'd a dog his hansel, an' he was hanged ere night.

An excuse for not giving a present or a favour.

I brought him aff the moor for God's sake, and he begins to bite the bairns.

Spoken when someone returns a favour with a disservice.

I canna sell the cow an' sup the milk.

'I cannot have my cake and eat it'.

I carena whether the fire gae about the roast, or the roast gae about the fire, if the meat be ready.

I do not care how, as long as the deed is done.

I deny that wi' baith hands and a' my teeth.

The most emphatic denial.

Idle young, needy auld.

If a lee could hae chokit you, ye wad hae been dead langsyne.

If a man's gaun down the brae, ilka ane gives him a jundie.

People rather enjoy seeing others falling on hard times.

If a' things are true, then that's nae lee.

You are lying.

If a' your hums an' haws were hams and haggises, the pairish would be weel fed.

Said to those who were indecisive.

**If Candlemas Day be dry an' fair,
The hauf o' winter's to come an' mair;
If Candlemas Day be wet an' foul,
The hauf o' winter's gane at Yule.**

Candlemas Day is 2nd February.

If he binds his pock, she'll sit down on't.

When a miserly man is married to an even more miserly woman.

If I come I maun bring my stool wi' me.

I haven't been invited, so there will be nowhere for me to sit.

If I had a dog as daft as you, I'd shoot him.

If it can be nae better, it's weel it's nae waur.

Making the best of it.

If ye dinna see the bottom, dinna wade.

Do not be reckless.

If ye sell your purse to your wife, gie her your breeks to the bargain.

If the wife is in charge of the money, she is in charge of everything including you.

It's a lang loanin' that has nae turnin'.

Things are bound to change.

It's an ill bird that files its ain nest.

Only an evil man would harm his own.

It's an ugly lass that's never kissed,
And a silly body that's never missed.

It's folly to live poor to dee rich.

Against miserliness.

It would be a hard task to follow a blackdockit soo through a burnt muir this nicht.

A vivid description of the darkness of certain nights.

I wouldna ken him if I met him in my parritch.

I have no idea who he is.

I would rather be your Bible than your horse.

Your Bible is not used much.

J

Jock's a mislear'd imp, but ye're a rum deil.

'Jock' is pretty mischievous, but nothing compared to you.

'John, John, pit your neck in the nick to please the laird'.

So a wife is said to have pleaded with her husband, who was resisting the laird's efforts to hang him. Applied to anyone who is offhand to his superiors.

Jouk an' let the jaw gang by.

Literally – take shelter until the shower blows over.
Accept what is inevitable and wait until it is over.

'Just as it fa's', quo the wooer to the maid.

The story has it that a young man dining with his girlfriend saw that she was serving supper with a drop on the end of her nose. She asked him if he would stay the night. He replied as above, meaning that if the drop fell into his supper he would leave – if it missed, he would stay.

Justice wrangs nae man.

K

Kame sindle, kame sair.

Literally – hair infrequently combed becomes difficult and painful to comb.
Necessary tasks neglected become troublesome.

Kamesters are aye creeshy.

Literally – wool-combers are always greasy.
People are always like their work.

Katie Sweerock, frae where she sat, cried, 'Reik me this, and reik me that'.

Applied to lazy people who get others to do their own jobs.

Keep a thing seven years and ye'll find a use for 't.

Keep out o' his company that cracks o' his cheatery.

Do not socialise with people who boast of their dishonesty.

Keep something for a sair fit.

Save it for a rainy day.

Keep woo', and it will be dirt; keep lint and it will be silk.

Flax improves with keeping, but wool rots.

Keep your breath to cool your parritch.

Spoken to those who have said too much too vehemently.

Keep your gab steekit when ye kenna your company.

Don't talk too freely when in strange company.

Keep your mocks till ye're married.

Keep your mou shut and your een open.

Kindle a candle at baith ends and it'll sune be dune.

Work and a hectic social life is bad for you.

Kings are kittle cattle to shoe behint.

Kings are not worthy of trust.

Kiss my foot, there's mair flesh on 't.

A retort to those who try to ingratiate themselves.

**Knock a carle, and ding a carle, and that's the way to win a carle;
Kiss a carle, and clap a carle, and that's the way to tine a carle.**

Boors are won over by rough treatment rather than kind.

Kythe in your ain colours, that folk may ken ye.

L

Lacking breeds laziness, but praise breeds pith.

A person discouraged will not strive, a person encouraged will.

Laith to bed, laith oot o't.

Lang and sma', gude for naething ava.

Jokingly applied to tall, thin people.

Lang lean maks hamald cattle.

Poorly kept cattle make ordinary meat.

Lang nint, little dint.

'Much ado about nothing.' Shakespeare.

Lang-tongued wives gang lang wi' bairn.

Don't tell everybody your plans unless you are sure they will work.

Lasses are like lamb-legs: they'll neither saut nor keep.

Make hay while the sun shines!

Law-makers shouldna be law-breakers.

Lean on the brose ye got in the morning.

Spoken facetiously to someone who relies heavily on another.

Learn young, learn fair; learn auld, learn mair.

Learn you an ill habit and ye'll ca 't a custom.

Leave aff while the play's gude.

Quit while the going is good.

Leein' rides on debt's back.

Lend your money and lose your friend.

With which there goes a rhyme:
I had a penny and a friend as many of this
    land,
I lent my penny to my friend when he did it
    demand,
I sought my penny from my friend when he
    had kept it long,
I lost my penny from my friend and was not
    that a' wrong?
Had I a penny and a friend as I have had
    before,
I wo'd keep my penny and my friend and
    play the fool no more.

Let ae deil dang anither.

An expression of indifference at two villains quarrelling.

Let the bell-wether brak the snaw.

The oldest sheep in the flock would wear a bell around its neck. The rest would follow it in difficult situations.

Listen to the voice of experience in an emergency.

Licht suppers mak lang days.

Liked gear is half-bought.

If you like something, you're half-way to buying it.

Little's the licht will be seen on a mirk nicht.

Lock your door, that ye may keep your neighbours honest.

Love ower het soon cools.

M

Maidens should be mim till they're married and then they may burn kirks.

'Anything goes' as long as you are married . . .

Maidens want naething but a man, and then they want a'thing.

It is just possible that this may still happen occasionally!

Mair by luck than by gude guiding.

A 'sour grapes' remark about someone's achievement.

Maister's will is gude wark.

For he is bound to be pleased with it.

Mak ae wrang step and down ye gae.

As one politician remarked to another.

Mak nae toom ruse.

Do not give empty praise.

Man's twal is no sae gude as the deil's dizzen.

Because 'man's twal' is twelve, while the 'deil's dizzen' is thirteen.

March comes wi' adders' heads and gangs wi' peacocks' tails.

Much preferable to 'comes like a lion and gangs like a lamb'. Anyway, a comment on weather in March.

Marriage and hanging gae by destiny.

Married folk are like rats in a trap – fain to get ithers in, but fain to be out themselves.

Maybe's a big book.

Maybe your pat will need my clips.

Maybe you will need my help one day (though you reject it now).

May he that turns the clod ne'er want a bannock.

In praise of honest toil.

Misterfu' folk mauna be mensefu'.

'Beggars should not be choosers'.

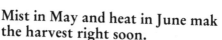

Mist in May and heat in June mak the harvest right soon.

Mistress before folk, gudewife behint backs, whaur lies the dishclout?

Jokingly applied to those who change their accent according to their surroundings.

Money's aye welcome, were it even in a dirty clout.

Money's like the muck midden, it does nae good till it be spread.

Mony a gude tale is spoilt in the telling.

Authority has it that this was often applied to sermons. Many other appropriate circumstances could be thought of, though.

Mony ane kisses the bairn for love o' its nurse.

Many do favours for those near to the one they love or respect, in order to gain favour.

Mony ane maks an errand to the ha' to bid my leddy good day.

Many fill their lives with 'trivial pursuits'.

Mony ane wad blush to hear what
he wadna blush to dae.

Mony littles mak a muckle.

'Must' is for the King to say.

N

Naebody is riving their claes to get you.

Nobody is worrying themselves unduly about you.

Nae faut; but she sets her bannet ower weel.

Her only fault is that she is too good-looking.

Nae gairdner ever lichtlied his ain leeks.

No man disparages what he considers most precious to him.

Nae man can baith sup and blaw at once.

No man can do two things at once.

Nae man can live longer in peace than his neighbours like.

Good neighbours are a blessing.

Nae man can thrive unless his wife will let him.

Naething comes fairer to licht than what has been lang hidden.

It is especially good to find things long lost.

Naething is got without pains but an ill name and lang nails.

Strive hard for what you want.

Naething like being stark deid.

Nothing like doing a thing thoroughly, but no doubt applied often enough in its literal sense upon hearing of an enemy's death.

Naething to be done in haste but grippin' fleas.

It is said that after an argument, one man handed the other what he thought was his card, so that they might duel over the question. On looking at the paper to discover his opponent's name, the other saw the above words instead. The effect was immediate reconciliation.

Naething to do but draw in your stool and sit down.

When a task is all but completed.

Nane can tell what's i' the shaup till it's shelt.

Near the kirk, but far frae grace.

Neck or naething, the king lo'es nae cripples.

If somebody might have an accident, this is a wish that they may either break their neck or escape completely, as any disability will make them a useless employee.

Ne'er do ill that gude may come o't.

The end does not necessarily justify the means.

Ne'er find faut wi' my shune, unless ye pay my soutar.

Don't criticise something you know nothing about.

Ne'er gie me my death in a toom dish.

If you want to kill me, don't do it by starvation, i.e. please feed me!

Ne'er let the nose blush for the sins o' the mouth.

Don't drink too much.

Ne'er look for a wife until ye hae a hoose and a fire to put her in.

Obviously some wives are not all they might be!

Ne'er misca' a Gordon in the raws of Strathbogie.

Don't criticise somebody in his friends' company.
There were many Gordons around Strathbogie.

Ne'er tak a stane to brak an egg, when ye can dae it wi' the back o' your knife.

Don't use unnecessary power to achieve a small end.

Next to nae wife, a gude ane's best.

O

O' a' ills, nane's best.

O' a little, tak a little; when there's nought, tak a'.

O' a' meat in the warld, the drink gaes best doon.

O' gude advisement comes nae ill.

Open confession is gude for the soul.

But not necessarily good for the body?

O' twa ills, choose the least.

Our sins and debts are often mair than we think.

A gloomy but prudent attitude.

Out o' Davy Lindsay into Wallace.

'Davy Lindsay' and 'Wallace' were school text-books. The saying was used when a person advanced from one thing to another.

Out o' the peat-pot into the gutter.

Out of the frying-pan into the fire.

Out o' the warld and into Kippen.

Kippen, near Stirling, was thought to be so out of the way that a visit to it was considered 'out o' the warld'. Used when going to any strange or remote place.

**'O, wad some power the giftie gie us
To see oorselves as ithers see us.'**

Robert Burns.

Ower mony cooks spoil the broth.

Ower mony irons i' the fire, some maun cool.

If somebody has too many projects in hand, some must fail.

Ower muckle loose leather about your chafts.

A rather rude way of saying somebody is looking too thin.

P

Patch and lang sit, build and soon flit.

A slow and careful rise is more likely to be permanent than a sudden one.

Penny wise and pound foolish.

Pigs may whistle, but they hae an ill mouth for't.

When a clumsy person is trying to do something he is unlikely to succeed at.

Placks and bawbees grow pounds.

Play carle wi' me again, if ye daur.

Argue with me if you dare. Usually used with cheeky children.

Pleading at the law is like fighting through a whin-bush – the harder the blows the sairer the scarts.

A comment on the tangled and tortuous processes of the law.

Plenty is nae plague.

Poor folk maun fit their wame to their winning.

Poor people often have to make do with a frugal diet.

Praise without profit puts little in the pat.

Pride and sweerdness need muckle uphauding.

Pride and laziness need a lot of maintaining.

Pride finds nae cauld.

Spoken when girls wore low-cut dresses.

Pride will hae a fa'.

Puddings and paramours should be hetly handled.

Love and puddings are unacceptable when they get cold.

Put your hand twice to your bannet for ance to your pouch.

You do well to be polite (lift your hat) always, and not pay quite so often.

Put your shanks in your thanks and mak gude gramashes o' them.

Literally – put your legs in your thanks and make good gaiters of them. Spoken to those who pay in thanks only.

Q

Quality without quantity is little thought o'.

Quey calves are dear veal.

Quick at meat, quick at wark.

Quick, for you'll ne'er be cleanly.

Do the job quickly, for you'll never do it neatly.

Quick returns mak rich merchants.

Quietness is best.

Hear, hear.

R

Raggit folk and bonny folk are aye ta'en haud o'.

Used jokingly when somebody has torn their clothing on some projection.

Raise nae mair deils than ye can lay.

Do not start anything you cannot stop.

Rather spoil your joke than tine your friend.

Rattan an moose
Lea' the puir woman's hoose;
Gang awa ower to the mill,
And there ane and a' ye'll get your fill.

Those whose homes were vermin-ridden wrote these lines on a wall, in the quaint hope that this would encourage the animals to leave.

Reckless youth maks ruefu' eild.

People who live recklessly when young, may regret it when they're old.

Remember, man, and keep in mind, a faithfu' friend is hard to find.

Riches are got wi' pain, kept wi' care and tint wi' grief.

Rich folk hae routh o' friends.

Rich people have plenty friends.

Right, Roger, sow's gude mutton.

Meaning, you are completely wrong.

Right wrangs nae man.

Rise when the day daws,
Bed when the nicht fa's.

Rodden tree and reid threid
Put the witches to their speed.

These were supposed to frighten off witches.

Royt lads may mak sober men.

Rule youth weel, for eild will rule itsel'.

S

Sair cravers are ill-payers.

Sairs shouldna be sair handled.
Be tactful in talking of delicate matters.

'Saut' quo' the souter when he had eaten a cow a' but the tail.
To encourage those who have nearly completed a job.

Say well and dae well end wi' ae letter,
Say well is gude, but dae well is better.

Scart-the-cog wad sup mair.
To 'scart the cog' is to scrape the bowl.

Scorn not the bush that beilds ye.
Do not despise your helpers.

Sel', sel' has half-filled hell.
Selfishness is the downfall of many.

Send your gentle blude to the market and see what it will buy.

Spoken to those who brag of their upper-class backgrounds.

Send you to the sea, and ye'll no get saut water.

Addressed to those whose intellect falls short of requirements.

Set a stoot hert to a stey brae.

Don't be discouraged by a difficult job.

She brak her elbow at the kirk door.

When marriage changes a girl into a lazy wife.

She frisks about like a cat's tail i' the sun.

Not necessarily a complimentary phrase.

She'll keep her ain side o' the house, and gang up and down yours.

Spoken of a woman thought to be too domineering.

She's black, but she has a sweet smack.

She's ugly, but she's rich.

She that fa's ower a strae's a tentless taupie.

It's a silly person who stumbles at the smallest obstacle.

Sodgers, fire and water soon mak room for themselves.

Some hae little sense, but ye're aye havering.

Sorrow and ill weather come unca'd.

One cannot influence these.

Speak o' the deil and he'll appear.

Spoken when someone appears when he has recently been the subject of conversation.

Speak weel o' the Hielands, but dwell in the Laigh.

Advice to inhabitants of the Laigh o' Moray not to speak a word against nor to try to live amongst Highlanders.

Steek your een and open your mou
And see what the King'll send ye.

A rhyme spoken to children when something to eat (usually nice) is to be put into their mouth.

Sticks and stanes may brak my banes,
But names'll never hurt me.

T

Tak awa Aiberdeen and twal mile roond and faar are ye?

Aberdonians think Aberdeen is the hub of the universe.

**That was the langsyne, when geese were swine
And turkeys chewed tobacco,
And sparrows bigget in auld men's beards,
And mowdies delved potatoes.**

Spoken when an unbelievable statement has been made.

'The best laid schemes o' mice and men gang aft agley.'

Robert Burns.

The breath of a fause friend's waur than the fuff o' a weasel.

The noise a weasel makes before it attacks is called fuffing. This would be an awful sound to hear, but even this, the proverb says, is better than 'the breath of a deceitful friend'.

The coo that's first up gets the first o' the dew.

The early bird catches the worm.

The deil's aye gude to his ain.

This expression would have had sinister implications at one time, but came to be used in fun.

The gravest fish is an oyster;
The gravest bird's an owl;
The gravest beast's an ass;
And the gravest man's a fule.

The king lies doun
Yet the warld rins roun.

Life goes on no matter what happens.

The loudest bummer's no the best bee.

The men o' the East
Are pykin their geese
And sendin their feathers here-
awa, there-awa.

A children's rhyme when snow fell.

The proof of the pudding is in the preein' o't.

There ne'er was a bad, but there micht be a waur.

There's aye some water whaur the stirkie droons.

There's no smoke without fire.
There must be a grain of truth in the story.

**There's nae airn sae hard but rust will fret it;
There's nae cloth sae fine but moths will eat it.**

Nothing is indestructible.

There's nocht for it but the twa thoombs.

This remark was overheard during the 1914-18 War, and was made by a soldier. Official efforts to delouse his battalion had failed. He advocated this fail-safe method – squashing the offending animals between the thumb-nails.

There's nocht sae queer as folk.

Nobody would disagree with this.

The siller penny slays mair souls than the nakit sword slays bodies.

Money is the root of all evil.

The tae hauf the warld thinks the tither hauf daft.

The willing horse is aye wrocht to daith.

This will strike a chord with any committee-member.

They hae need o' a canny cook that hae but ae egg to their denner.

The Scots are no strangers to frugality.

They wha hae a gude Scots tongue in their heid are fit to gang ower the warld.

There will always be an expatriate Scot to whom one can talk wherever one is.

They wha pay the piper hae a richt tae ca' the tune.

They're fremit friends that canna be fashed.

Think mair than ye say.

Truth and honesty keep the croon o' the causey.

The 'croon o' the causey' was the highest and therefore cleanest part of the street. Those who considered themselves worthy and respectable would walk there, leaving the rest to make do with the filthy and stinking gutter.

U

Under water dearth, under snaw bread.

A crop drenched with rain will be spoiled, but a crop covered with snow will be protected.

Unseen, unrued.

Untimeous spurring spoils the steed.

Use maks perfyteness.

Practice makes perfect.

W

Wad ye gar us trow that the mune's made o' green cheese, or that spade shafts bear plooms?

How can you expect anyone to believe such a story?

Waes unite faes.

Waly, waly! bairns are bonny; ane's enough and twa's ower mony.

Want o' cunning's nae shame.

Cunning is no virtue.

War makes thieves and peace hangs them.

War's sweet tae them that never tried it.

War seems glorious until you are fighting.

Wealth has made mair men covetous than covetousness has made men wealthy.

We are a' life-like and death-like.

We can live without our kin, but no without our neighbours.

We can poind for debt, but no for unkindness.

We can shape their wylie-coat, but no their weird.
We can influence a person's appearance but not his destiny.

Wedding and ill wintering tame baith man and beast.

Weel begun is half done.

Welcome's the best dish in the kitchen.

We'll meet ere hills meet.
i.e. never.

Wha daur bell the cat?

A famous Scots saying. A mouse suggested hanging a bell around the cat's neck to warn of his approach. A more worldly-wise mouse then asked the above.

Scots history has a well-known application of the proverb. Some Scottish nobles met to decide how to deal with one of the favourites of James III. They wanted to hang him, but Lord Gray asked 'Wha daur bell the cat?' The Earl of Angus took up the challenge, succeeded and was known thereafter as Archibald Bell-the-Cat.

What maks you sae rumgunshach and me sae curcuddoch?

Why are you so rude when I only want to please you?

What's in your wame's no in your testament.

Said to encourage somebody to eat more. They won't be leaving what they eat in their will.

When ye can suit your shanks to my shune ye may speak.

When you are in my position you can competently speak on the subject.

Y

Ye breed o' the gowk, ye hae ne'er a rhyme but ane.

You always talk about the same thing.

Ye breed o' the tod, ye grow grey before ye grow gude.

Ye canna get leave to thrive for thrang.

You are so busy, you have no time to get rich.

Ye canna hae mair o' a soo than a grumph.

Don't expect more than is reasonable.

Ye canna make a silk purse oot o' a soo's lug.

Ye canna pit an auld heid on young shoulders.

Ye crack crousely wi' your bannet on.

Said to somebody too forward in his manner.

Ye cut lang whangs aff ither folk's leather.

You are very generous with other people's property.

Ye didna lick your lips since ye leed last.

Spoken to an habitual liar.

Ye fand it where the Hielandman fand the tongs.

You stole it. A reply to those who claim to have 'found' something. You 'found' it in its proper place, where it should stay.

Ye fike it awa', like auld wives baking.

You waste time by fussing.

Ye hae come in time to tine a darg.

You have come too late.

Ye hae grown proud since ye quatted the begging.

A satirical remark addressed to those who walk past their acquaintances haughtily.

Ye'll be a man afore your mither.

A promise made to small boys.

Ye'll get waur bodes ere Beltane.

Spoken to those who have refused a 'good' offer or bid for something.

Ye shape shune by your ain shauchled feet.

You judge everyone by your own low standards.

Ye wad wheedle a laverock frae the lift.

You are very persuasive.

Yule is young on Yule even, and auld on Saint Stephen.

Glossary

Glossary

a'	all
advisement	advice, counsel
ae	one
aff	off
afore	before
agley	amiss, off the straight
ahint	behind
ain	own
airn	iron
aiver	old horse
ance	once
ava	at all
aye	always
bairn	child
baith	both
bannet	bonnet, hat
bannock	oatcake
bauld	bold
bawbee	halfpenny
behint	behind
beild	shelter
beit	to renew, kindle
bell-wether	the oldest sheep in the flock
Beltane	a May festival
buid	restrain
bink	bench, seat; shelf
bite	food
black	grimy; foul
black-dockit	black-bottomed
blate	bashful, shy
blaw	to blow
blude	blood
blythe	happy
bode	(n) bid, price, offer; (v) to signify; foretell

bonnet	hat
brae	hillside
brak	break
breed	to resemble, take after
breeks	trousers
breid	bread
brither	brother
broo	broth; juice
brose	porridge, oatmeal mixed with boiling water
brugh	the halo around the sun or moon
bubbly-jock	turkey-cock
bum	to buzz
buskit	made ready, adorned
byre	cow-shed
ca'	to call, invite
caff and draff	inferior quality grain
canna	cannot
canny	cautious, careful
care	worry, concern
carena	do not care
carle	boor
carlin	old woman
cauld	cold
causey	causeway, street
chafts	cheeks
chancy	lucky
change	ale-house, tavern
chiel	fellow
claes	clothes
clean	neat, well-made
cloot, clout	garment
cluse	shut
cog	bowl
cooper	dealer
counts	sums, accounts
crack	conversation

craik	to complain
craver	creditor
craw	rook; the crowing of a cock
creep	to crawl
crook	hook, device; river's bend
croon	the top of anything; the roar of a bull
crouse	bold, lively, confident
curcuddoch	kindly
dae	to do
daffin	sport, play
daft	giddy, silly
daidle	to dawdle
daith	death
dang	to knock, bang
darg	a day's work
daw	to dawn
dawt	to caress, pet
dee	to die
deid	dead
deil	devil
denner	dinner
dike	wall
ding	to smash, cut down
dink	neat, trim
dinna	do not
dint	blow, shock
dit	to close
dish-clout	dish-cloth
divot	turf
dizzen	dozen
dool	sorrow, misfortune
douce	kind, gentle, respectable
dozen	to fade, become spiritless
draff	inferior grain
drap	drink
droon	to drown
dune	down; done, exhausted

ee(n)	eye(s)
eild	age; old age
eith	easy
ell	about a yard
eneugh	enough
even	evening, eve
fa'	(n) fall; (v) to fall
faar	where
fae	foe, enemy
fain	eager, anxious
fair	completely; accurately
fair fa'	good luck to
fash	to trouble, inconvenience
fause	false, deceitful
faut	fault, blame
feckless	weak in mind, irresponsible
fike	to fuss, waste time
file	to defile
fit	(n) foot; (v) to add up
flee	(n) fly; (v) to fly
fleech	to flatter
flit	to move house
forgie	to forgive
frae	from
freend	friend
fremit	strange
fret	to eat, devour
fu'	drunk, tipsy
fuff	spitting, puffing
gab	mouth
gairdner	gardener
gaislin	gosling
gane	gone
gang	to walk, go
gar	to make, cause
gate	way, route
gaun	going
gaunt	to yawn

gaylie	pretty well
gear	money, wealth, property
gentle	well-born, noble
ghaist	ghost
gie	to give
giff-gaff	giving and taking, reciprocity
girn	to moan, complain
glaiket	deceitful
glib	cunning, smooth-tongued
glum	sullen, moody
gowd	gold
gowk	fool; cuckoo
graith	harness for horses
gramashes	gaiters
greet	to cry
grip	to catch
grosset	gooseberry
grumph	grunt
gryce	young pig
gude-wife	housewife
ha'	the chief manor-house
hae	to have
hain	to save
hamald	homely, domestic; common
hame	home
hansel	gift
haud	to hold, keep to oneself
hauf	half
haver	to talk nonsense
haw	hawthorn berry
heid	head
hert	heart
het	hot
ilka	each
ill	bad, unkind
ither	other
jaw	shower

jouk	to stoop
jundie	push, shove
kail	broth
kame	to comb
kebbuck	cheese
keep	to watch over
ken	to know
kindle	to light
kindly	natural, in good condition
kirn	churn
kirk	church
kittle	uncertain; cunning
kythe	to appear, show oneself
lack	to slight
laird	lord, landed proprietor
laith	loath
langsyne	long ago
laverock	lark
lay	to put down
leather	skin
leave aff	to stop
leddy	lady
lee	(n) lie; (v) to lie
licht	light; frugal
lichtlie	to make light of, disparage
lichtsome	pleasant, delightful
life-like and death-like	used of the uncertainty of life
lift	sky
linn	the ledge over which a waterfall pours
lint	flax
lip	a device for lifting a pot from the fire
loanin'	lane
loe	to love
loose	louse
lowe	flame, glow

lowp	to leap
lug	ear
mair	more
maun	must
mensefu'	discreet, well-mannered
micht	might
mim	demure, prim
mint	to insinuate, hint
mirk	dark
misca'	to speak evil of
mislear'd	mischievous, ill-mannered
misterfu'	needy, poor
mither	mother
mock	jest, joke
mony	many
mou	mouth
muck	worthless; dirty
muckle	much; large
muck-midden	dunghill
muir	moor, heath
na	not
nae	no
nakit	naked
neb	nose
nicht	night
nick	noose
no	not
nocht	nought, nothing
nowte	black cattle
oo	wool
ower	too, over
painting	application of cosmetics
pairish	parish, district
parritch	porridge
pat	pot
pawky	shrewd; dry

peat-pot	hole from which peat has been dug
perfyteness	exactness, perfection
pit	to put
pith	substance; marrow
plack	a small coin
play-carle again	to give as good as one gets
ploom	plum
pock	wallet
poind (pronounced pind)	to seize a debtor's property
poortith	poverty
pouch	(n) wallet, purse; (v) to steal, pocket
pree	to taste, eat
preen	pin
pyke	to pick, pluck
quat	to quit, stop
quey	a heifer until she has had calves
quo, quoth	said
raggit	ragged
raw	row, ridge
reid	red
reik	to reach
riggin'	roof-top
rin	to run
ripplin'-kame	coarse comb used in the preparation of flax
rive	to tear
Rodden	mountain-ash, rowan
roun	around
routh	plenty
royt	to drift aimlessly or idly
rum	wicked
rumgunshach	coarse, rude, unkind
run	(short for runagate) (adj) vagabond; (n) worthless person

ruse	praise, flattery
sae	so
Saint Stephen	Boxing Day
sair	sore; great; expensive
sark	shirt, chemise
saut	salt
scart	(n) scratch; (v) to scrape
scaud	to scald
scraggy	thin, spare
sel'	self
set	to set, place
shanks	legs
shape	to cut out, plan
shauchle	to shuffle
shaup	shell
shochel	to hobble
shoe	to shoe
shune	shoes
sic	such
sicker	secure, safe
siller	money, silver
sindle	seldom
sliddry	slippery
sma'	small
smack	kiss
snaw	snow
sober	steady
sodger	soldier
soo	sow
soucht	sought
soutar, souter	cobbler, shoe-maker
speir	to ask
spune	spoon
stane	stone
steek	(n) stitch; (v) to shut
stey	steep
stirkie	little steer

stoor	dust
stoot	stout, strong
strae	straw
sune	soon
sup	to eat
sweerdness	laziness
tae	the one contrasted with the other
tak haud o'	to take hold of
talla	grease, fat
taupie	foolish woman
tentless	careless
testament	will
thegither	together
thoomb	thumb
thrang	pressure of work; business
tine	to lose
tint	lost
tither	the other
tod	fox
toom	empty
trew	to trust, believe
trow	to make one believe
turn	to change
turnin'	corner
twa	two
twal	twelve
unca'd	uncalled
uphaud	to support, uphold
wad	would
wae	sorrowful
wame	stomach
wan	won
warld	world
waukrife	wakeful
weel	well, happy
weird	destiny, fate

wersh	tasteless
whang	thong, long strip of leather
whaur	where
whelp	silly man
whin-bush	gorse
wispit	rubbed down, cleaned
wrang	to wrong
wrocht	worked
wylie-wat	flannel shirt
yett	gate
Yule	Christmas